Kind Karma Worldwide™

Inspirational Quotes & Empowering Thoughts for Raising the Vibration of Humanity

A Humanitarian Non-Profit 501(c)(3) Organization

Original Quotes Created By:
Dean Telano, Ph.D.
Founder of Kind Karma Worldwide™

Kind Karma Worldwide™

Inspirational Quotes & Empowering Thoughts for Raising the Vibration of Humanity

Author: Dean Telano, Ph.D.
Founder of Kind Karma Worldwide™ & Kind Karma® Yoga
Creator of Awaken Qigong & Awaken with Meditation

Edited by: Emma Jaeger
Published by: Kind Karma Publications

Kind Karma Worldwide™
Humanitarian Nonprofit 501(c)(3) Organization

<u>www.kindkarmaworldwide.org</u>

ISBN 978-0-9846625-0-0
Printed in the United States of America

DEDICATION

To my wife, Naomi, who is as beautiful as the day I met her. Truly the North Star in my life, forever guiding me with her divine radiance and unparalleled angel spark. Through her everlasting inspiration and deep insightful nature, the quotes found inside this book, that were once only a dream, are now part of the fabric of reality.

ACKNOWLEDGMENTS

A special thank you to Emma Jaeger, who edited this book, for her fine editing expertise, along with her creative thinking and critical analysis skills.

I would also like to extend a high vibrational thank you to Heidi Zeller and Lauren Merlino for their time and effort in collecting my quotes.

Kind Karma Worldwide™

Mission

As a humanitarian nonprofit organization, Kind Karma Worldwide™ was created to propagate positivity and high vibrational energies to help usher in a new earth awakening.

Our international mission is to raise the consciousness and vibration of humanity through its holistic initiatives, empowerment programs and community events.

We are shaping our world's future by empowering the present.

We welcome your support and contributions to the Kind Karma Worldwide community as we collaborate and engage, to emerge stronger.

Vision

Kind Karma® Initiatives are designed to have a profound impact on your life, how you connect with others, and how you view and care for the world. The initiatives are intended to create positive outcomes and high vibrational energies through 'mind-body' courses, 'holistic and integrative health' workshops, and inspirational 'raise your vibration' events. We are creating a global canvas and person to person empowerment landscape for harmony, peace, respect and kindness.

Goals

Kind Karma's goal is to create a worldwide community where people are empowered to develop the skills and self-awareness to enable positive change in their communities, families and in themselves. Starting with each person, Kind Karma Worldwide™ is about taking positive steps and actions to raise humanity's vibrational energies towards a brighter future. If each person can accomplish this, we believe, will see less: violence and hostility; injustice and bullying; unhappiness; and animal and environmental abuse.

Table of Contents

Kind Karma Quote #1

Loving Kindness in Action

"I believe 'loving kindness' is contained inside our human DNA; it's our shared genetic spirituality and connectivity. We are born with this KIND of DNA (I call it, 'Cosmic Coding'), and hence it's our birthright, as well as human and spiritual obligation, to 'act' upon it.
When we approach our own lives from authentic loving kindness – and resonate with this TRUTH – we have the infinite ability, potential, and desire to make positive, beautiful, and inspiring changes in the world."

Kind Karma Quote #2

Kind Karma's Formula for Success

"Often our voice is found in our compassionate actions."

Kind Karma Quote #3

Random vs. Mindful Acts of Kindness

"Yes, there is a natural beauty to 'random' acts of kindness. However, with MINDFUL acts of kindness, there is a shared empowering beauty, awakening, and enlightenment. This creates a diamond sparkle – scintillation, and an ineffable dimension to our being."

Kind Karma Quote #4

We all have Magic Inside Us

"Do not settle for ordinary living and mundane moments when there is extraordinary magic within you."

Kind Karma Quote #5

Grace

"Teaching kindness is the same as teaching grace. Both emanate from God's love and radiance."

Kind Karma Quote #6

Living Consciously

"Become the type of kindness you want to experience in the world around you."

Kind Karma Quote #7

I am the Power

"My inner space is my power space."

Kind Karma Quote #8

Reflect the Light of Truth

"Upon each day's awakening, we are reborn into a new life. It is up to us to live it as such."

Kind Karma Quote #9

We are Suns

*"Every moment you give kindness, you
instantaneously create a kinder world."*

Kind Karma Quote #10

Endless. Infinite. Limitless.

"Kindness, love, and compassion allow the impossible to become possible."

Kind Karma Quote #11

A Blessing in Disguise

"An act of kindness is a 'blessing' incognito."

Kind Karma Quote #12

Divine Graces

"Kind Karma® is part of the wave crest of the Celestial Sound Current, which is the vibratory sound breath of God, restoring and replenishing life. So remain current, be one with the ocean, and mindfully ride the wave of Divine Graces of Kind Karma."

Kind Karma Quote #13

Kind Karma is Loving Kindness

"To express love is to know kindness. To express kindness is to know love. Both are a blessed extension of one another."

Kind Karma Quote #14

Dancing with a Kind Karma Heart

"The most magical dance party is when you invite Kindness, Compassion, and Love. They are the perfect dance partners – never to step on anybody's toes, because they move from the Heart first."

Kind Karma Quote #15

The Great Kind Karma Harvest

"Tend the field of your heart, for seeds of kindness, love, and compassion faithfully await. A flowering trinity of spiritual bliss longing for nourishment by your own luminous familiarity."

Kind Karma Quote #16

Inviolability

"A Kind Karma awakening is about realizing the significance of love, compassion, empathy, and kindness. The composed quartet are one inseparable whole. They are only separated through convenience of mind and persuasion of flavor, not of Divine Love or illuminated wisdom."

Kind Karma Quote #17

One-Way Trip to Kind Karma

"One day, the Winged Horse of Loving Kindness swooped down and approached me, and said: 'Awaken, and let's go!'
I got into the saddle (or, was it... 'back' into the saddle?), and flew into the softness of the vast blue sky, never regretting."

Kind Karma Quote #18

Blissful Trinity of Infinity

"The heart that has been opened by the Blissful Trinity of Kindness, Love, and Compassion, has the potential to create infinite possibilities for changing the world."

Kind Karma Quote #19

Without Regret

"Awakened, I had decided to devote myself to God, and haven't regretted it since."

Kind Karma Quote #20

When the Word is Heard

"Prayer has its greatest potency not in recitation of words, or committed sustained efforts, or familiar comforts, but in who is listening to you. When you begin to feel that the Listener is fully present and in the moment with you — the true power of worship — your heart will throb and swell with the spiritual vibrations of glory, joy, bliss, peace, faith, love, compassion, and kindness."

Kind Karma Quote #21

An Instrument of God

"Embark upon the great crusade of untying the knots of your heart, and then shall you begin to realize both love and kindness belong to the same eternal, vibrating, cosmic-stringed instrument of God."

Kind Karma Quote #22

Internal Hymn of Kind Karma®

*"Devoted ones, give ear to your own heartstrings.
Smoothly pluck to create God's music.
Rejoice with laughter, song and dance.
Celebrate – and give a smile and praise to the
enduring hymn of: 'Forever Loving-Kindness.'"*

Kind Karma Quote #23

God's Gateway

"Open, align, and cultivate your heart's qualities with a true intention and honest motivation, and enter through the Spiritual Gateway of God that lovingly awaits you."

Kind Karma Quote #24

God's Love is the Antidote

"Viruses are Godless and loveless. Those are their sustaining powers. Therefore, the first responders should include God and Love."

Kind Karma Quote #25

Head Chef

"Don't be hesitant to stir the pot. Often, it's a necessity. How else are you going to create a homogenous mixture, disperse temperature, and reveal the hidden aroma?"

Kind Karma Quote #26

Do You Believe in Miracles?

"Sing and praise kindness, and you will bear witness to multitudes of miracles every day."

Kind Karma Quote #27

Set Your Sights

"There are consequential moments in our lives where we need to see with our heart, not our eyes."

Kind Karma Quote #28

Heart Failure

"When you are too much in your own head, you are losing time of being in your own heart."

Kind Karma Quote #29

Empowering our Future

"If we want to create a better world future, we must teach our children about the law of karma, or the importance of being responsible and accountable for their actions or lack thereof."

Kind Karma Quote #30

Déjà vu

"There's no better tomorrow than today."

Kind Karma Quote #31

Parallel Universe

"You make the impossible possible only when you strive for the impossible."

Kind Karma Quote #32

Allowing 'What Is'

"We are most powerful when we are calm, yielding, and relaxed."

Kind Karma Quote #33

The Power of Three

"Kindness, compassion, and love contain unique elements intersecting at our chest, what we call our heart center. Together, at this junction, the combined Spiritual Trinity vibrates, giving birth to the beautiful physical and energetic 'heart-shape' symbol. This means to truly HAVE HEART, one needs to create three ways to make room for kindness, compassion and love."

Kind Karma Quote #34

Gaia

"The earth is our loving mother. Together, let's feel her pulse; see her beauty; hear her song; dance to her music; and cherish her breath."

Kind Karma Quote #35

We are not Alone

"We all belong to the celestial kingdom of loving kindness."

Kind Karma Quote #36

You are the Gatekeeper of your Own Life

"We can create and shape the future of our own lives by taking action and empowering the present moment."

Kind Karma Quote #37

Set Your Sails

"Kindness is personified ambivalence when not acted upon by a mind that's not moved in the right direction by the inward winds of compassion."

Kind Karma Quote #38

Bye, Bye, Negative Self!

"Become more, challenge adversity."

Kind Karma Quote #39

'Nose-to-Nose' Finish

"I think we live by inches. We just don't realize it, or barely think about it until the distance suddenly decreases, and cold shivers run up along the spine with an unexpected and loss of life sustaining wind."

Kind Karma Quote #40

Aparigraha

"Giving without the expectation of receiving anything back, will heal your heart, nourish your soul and bring you closer to God."

Kind Karma Quote #41

Mother Awareness

"Gratitude is God's Grace."

Kind Karma Quote #42

Braveheart

*"Living a life of kindness is supremely profound,
breathtaking, and a noble path of the Heart."*

Kind Karma Quote #43

Heart Lotus

"Speaking kindly, with sweet tenderness, will water and nourish the Lotus Flower in your Heart Center."

Kind Karma Quote #44

Joy of Effort

"Kindness gladdens the heart."

Kind Karma Quote #45

℞

"Gratitude is a natural steroid for enlarging our Heart. The only side effects are love, compassion and kindness."

Kind Karma Quote #46

Positive Daily Affirmation

*"If you want to change the world, live by these words:
'Loving-kindness begins with me.'"*

Kind Karma Quote #47

Maitreya

"Kind Karma Worldwide™ is Global Metta Medicine."

Kind Karma Quote #48

Immeasurable Whole

"When we heal a part in and of ourselves, we also heal that part in the world."

Kind Karma Quote #49

The Key is Hidden Under the Mat

"Empowering the world with 'Kind Karma®' is one of the keys to unlock the door of compassion and open the window of wisdom."

Kind Karma Quote #50

Heart Whisperer

"Sometimes the most meaningful, audible whispers are not heard by the ear, but with the heart."

Kind Karma Quote #51

Divine Refulgence

"Frequently, hidden in the murky depths of desolation and desperation, awaits an unexpected sparkle of inspiration, regeneration and hope."

Kind Karma Quote #52

Divine Attitude

"A true action is rooted in an authentic intention."

Kind Karma Quote #53

Aim Higher than the Stars

*"A soaring heart always maintains the highest
spiritual altitude."*

Kind Karma Quote #54

Caution: Harmonic Currents

"If you complicate simple things, then it becomes simply complicated."

Kind Karma Quote #55

Sweet, Heavenly Essence

"Being kind is not the latest trend or something we need to achieve. It's part of the inherent beauty of who we already are."

Kind Karma Quote #56

Earn your Wings

"Proper attitude allows for proper altitude."

Kind Karma Quote #57

Self-Liberation. Naked Awareness.

"Sometimes the path of redundancy leads us to the path of awareness, awakening, and eventual freedom."

Kind Karma Quote #58

Quench your Spiritual Thirst

"A heart that has been desiccated can be quenched by the healing waters of love, compassion, and kindness."

Kind Karma Quote #59

Breakout

"Step out of your all-too-familiar comfort zone if you want to become more, discover more, and share more."

Kind Karma Quote #60

Authenticity

"Dear Truth Seekers, sometimes the high road is not the right road."

Kind Karma Quote #61

Kind Karma® Music to My Ears

"The chord of kindness, compassion, and love is the musical key that opens our heart."

Kind Karma Quote #62

5G. ?G.

"Ahhh... sweet, sweet tasting gossip.
Please, unlock the chains that imprison me.
Untangle my face gloss up.
Will you set me free?
A laughter not so sincere.
A forged smile soon to disappear.
Not kind to the ears.
Only later, heartaches and tears.
A mouth of decay and rot.
A life-saving breath I'm not.
Love only to evaporate and disappear.
The fires of compassion are extinguished and no
longer here.
Oh gossip, remove your entranced spell.
I plead with you, unlock the door of my cell."

Kind Karma Quote #63

Lost in Space

"If you remain on the path, and falter or fall, you will get up while still being on the path. If you are not on the path, if you falter or fall, you will get up disoriented, and lost."

Kind Karma Quote #64

En-amored

"The only 'arms' race should be the one where we walk, together, hand in hand."

Kind Karma Quote #65

Inborn Capacity

"Kindness and compassion can do the impossible, they can occupy the same space at the same time. This impossibility made possible should call to mind our innate 'wholeness' and inspire us to act upon it 'wholeheartedly'."

Kind Karma Quote #66

Just Married

"If not motivated by the sincere goodwill to serve others, a spiritual divorce between compassion and kindness is inevitable."

Kind Karma Quote #67

Matrimony

"When KINDNESS weds COMPASSION, inherently, the treasured officiant is LOVE."

Kind Karma Quote #68

All for One, and One for All

"Love is beautiful, romantic, and should be something we breathe, live, and freely – share."

Kind Karma Quote #69

Go Toward the Light

"Light is Might because it's God's Radiance of Love."

Kind Karma Quote #70

Mirror, Mirror on the Wall

"Not only do we see the world with our eyes, but we also see it from our heart.
What do you see?"

Kind Karma Quote #71

Faith

"The climb is not in the height, it's in the belief."

Kind Karma Quote #72

Inner Peaks

---

*"To overcome the most menacing mountain range,
you must first mount the inner landscape of yourself."*

Kind Karma Quote #73

We are in Control

"Good news and bad news: Kind Karma® is a results-oriented, driven institution."

Kind Karma Quote #74

My Favorite Song

"Peace, joy, happiness, love and compassion are all expressed through the radiant abode of melody, dance and music of kindness."

Kind Karma Quote #75

Macro-Kindness

"Even the smallest acts of kindness will make such big differences."

Kind Karma Quote #76

Sorry, We are Closed Today

"There is no catch-up. There are only lost opportunities with visitation rights revoked."

Kind Karma Quote #77

Who Are You Becoming?

*"Be of action that leads to a well sought out manifestation.
A day wasted is a future lost."*

Kind Karma Quote #78

Essence of Ultimate Truth

"The blossoming of self-arising awareness allows for the metamorphosis of heart energy to Divine energy."

Kind Karma Quote #79

Ultimate Renewable Energy Source

"Our soul-flower power is found inside each of our hearts. Its natural turbines are generated by the loving electricity of kindness and strong inner winds of compassion."

Kind Karma Quote #80

Excuses, Excuses, Excuses

"I think in the entire world, including nature herself and all her living beings, humans are the only ones who make excuses."

Kind Karma Quote #81

Wisdom of Lift-to-Drag Ratio

"Kindness, love, and compassion work together to maximize lift and minimize drag. Accordingly, it's best to have all three when you are all ready to set sail for world change."

Kind Karma Quote #82

Unhooking and Releasing

"The consistent practice of releasing and letting go of what no longer serves you is a wonderful opportunity to catch what you are missing."

Kind Karma Quote #83

Turn your Dream into Reality

"A dream becomes a reality only when you decide to act upon it."

Kind Karma Quote #84

Hridya

"Benevolence does not come from the brain; it emanates from the heart – the reflection waters of one's own life."

Kind Karma Quote #85

Kind Karma® is Contagious

"When you act from an open heart motivated with loving kindness, the heart of the recipient will swell and open as well."

Kind Karma Quote #86

Kind Karma Worldwide™

*"Compassion, gratitude, and Kind Karma® walk
hand-in-hand to help heal the hearts of the world."*

Kind Karma Quote #87

Kind Karma Worldwide™

"Love, compassion, kindness, peace, empathy, and respect are SOUL-U-tions for a better world."

Kind Karma Quote #88

Kind Karma Worldwide™

"Togetherness will spontaneously arise when we spread Kind Karma Worldwide™."

Kind Karma Quote #89

Kind Karma Worldwide™

*"Kind Karma Worldwide™ is about:
'__M__otivation; __E__mpowerment; __I__nspiration'
(__MEI__, means beauty)."*

Kind Karma Quote #90

Kind Karma Worldwide™

"Love is light, and light is love. So, LIGHT this world up with some LOVE."

Kind Karma Quote #91

Kind Karma Worldwide™

"You never have to worry about creating negative karma if you flourish in Kind Karma®."

Kind Karma Quote #92

Kind Karma Worldwide™

*"Kind Karma's Worldwide™ superpower is loving kindness.
What's your superpower?"*

Kind Karma Quote #93

Kind Karma Worldwide™ *Initiatives*

"Kind Karma Worldwide™ *four initiatives are created to change and raise your daily personal vibration. When you raise your vibration, your life changes and the world transforms right before your eyes, leading to a fulfilled life guided from your authentic-self."*

Kind Karma Quote #94

Kind Karma Worldwide™ Initiatives

"Kind Karma Worldwide™ initiatives are imbued with a soul essence connection that encourages one to recognize and acknowledge what's necessary for world change. Each initiative is interspersed with Divine Love, Spiritual Light of Hope, Divination of Grace, and the Divine Utterances of Kindness."

Kind Karma Quote #95

Kind Karma® Creators

"Kind Karma® Creators are light lamps, spreading our light through positive deeds and actions. Allowing our heart whispers to be heard, we are here to shine our light in holistic ways, inspiring others to unite and join the Mission of Oneness."

Kind Karma Quote #96

Mindful Awakened Awareness (MAA)

"React less, adapt more, and respond with positivity or evenness."

Kind Karma Quote #97

Mindful Awakened Awareness (MAA)

"Kind Karma's groundwork is not just random acts of kindness but rather, 'mindful acts of kindness'. This refined strength of kindness is what Kind Karma® is about, and it's the prerequisite to stop and reverse the negative tide of karma that has already been created. A mindful, present Kind Karma act – in thought, word and deed, will always bear healthy fruit for both givers and receivers to counter a future of negative karma."

Kind Karma Quote #98

Mindful Awakened Awareness (MAA)

"To change your current life recipe, and to create a better future, stock your mental, emotional and spiritual pantry with plenty of essential, high vibration ingredients."

Kind Karma Quote #99

Mindful Awakened Awareness (MAA)

"Mindfulness is about the moment, the state of awareness, and presence of mind you carry along with it."

Kind Karma Quote #100

Mindful Awakened Awareness (MAA)

"There are no 'small gestures of kindness' because each one is intrinsically imbued with immeasurable value and worth. The essence of each kind gesture stands on its own merit, waiting to be fulfilled as a boundless, unexpected grace of compassion and connection for someone... somewhere."

Kind Karma Quote #101

Mindful Awakened Awareness (MAA)

"The practice of Kind Karma® – creating and cultivating loving kindness karma, helps to illuminate our vision as to what is no longer serving us, so we can truly serve ourselves and be in 'kind' service to others. In this way, we share the same source fabric of what is now popularly known as, YOGA."

Kind Karma Quote #102

Kind Karma® Cares Initiative

(HAH – <u>H</u>olistic <u>A</u>nimal <u>H</u>ealing)
"It's our belief that learning how to heal and properly care for animals contributes to simultaneously healing yourself and the planet. Hence, we are on a global mission to heal all types of animals, including birds, fish, reptiles, and amphibians."

Kind Karma Quote #103

Kind Karma® Cares Initiative

(HAH – <u>H</u>olistic <u>A</u>nimal <u>H</u>ealing)
"Animals, birds, fish, reptiles, amphibians and insects are undertaking a soul mission on earth just as we humans are. Through this shared soul mission, we are spiritually connected."

Kind Karma Quote #104

Planet Kind Karma® Initiative

(Healing, Honoring and Caring for our Planet, Mother Earth)
"Communicating and honoring the tree, plant, flower and herb spirits will help us, collectively, become aware of the Unity of All Life."

Kind Karma Quote #105

Planet Kind Karma® Initiative

*(Healing, Honoring and Caring for our Planet,
Mother Earth)*
*"Out from the love, compassion and kindness of
Mother Earth,*
bask in the glow of the bright, luminous moonlight.
*Reminding you to find your inner compass that points
towards the light.*
*New beginnings will emerge, boarding the shuttle, and
taking flight.*
With the destination in your sight."

Kind Karma Quote #106

Planet Kind Karma® Initiative: Earth Gifting

"Planet Kind Karma® uses the term, 'Earth Gifting' to inspire others how to 'gift' healing energy, compassion and gratitude to our planet, Earth. Earth Gifting is our holistic solution to a healthy Earth and a wonderful opportunity to simultaneously connect with nature and lead an environmental stewardship to protect and heal our planet."

Kind Karma Quote #107

Planet Kind Karma® Initiative
Spoken Word from the Fey of the Greens

"Give ear to me: calm your mind, heal your heart, harmonize your soul and soothe your spirit, and so shall kindness spontaneously arise."
– Channeled by Dr. Dean Telano

Kind Karma Quote #108

Planet Kind Karma® Initiative
Kind Karma® Gnome Prayer of Gratitude

Authored by Dr. Dean Telano

"Dear Gnomes,
The earth dwellers, wisdom sages and guardians of Mother
Earth and her:

> *secret treasures;*
> *plants, flowers and trees;*
> *animals of all kind;*
> *internal and external landscapes;*
> *crystals and gemstones;*
> *energy centers and ley lines or dragon's tracks;*
> *and all that belongs to her and all that she has given,*
> *and yet to give, birth to.*

With kindness and gratitude, we ask for your wisdom lamp
knowledge, good fortune, and dancing light guidance, today,
for our 'Planet Kind Karma® Earth Gifting' event.
We call upon you to impart your kinship, prowess, ingenuity,
jovial and peaceful nature, and earth magic to guide us along
our mission of propagating Kind Karma Worldwide.
Dearest kind Gnomes, with heart light sincerity, we pay
homage to the Gnome Lineage, Ancients and Realm, and we
thank you for your countless blessings."
Amor Vincit Omnia – Love Conquers All

Kind Karma Quote #109

Planet Kind Karma® Initiative

"Kind Karma® values nature connectedness and healing the planet with sacred moments."

Planet Kind Karma® Initiative
Blessed Faery

"The Light of the Faery beautifies our inner world and helps us to perceive the unacquainted magic that surrounds us every moment of our life."

Planet Kind Karma® Initiative
Kind Karma® Fairy Prayer of Gratitude

Authored by Dr. Dean Telano

"Dear Sweetest, Most Kind Faeries,
The 'children' of the mystic lights of the sublime realm of self-liberation.
The infinite 'generators' of the iridescent glow and nature spirit
unfathomable.
The 'flying alchemists' of the crystal ray realm.
The 'authors' of the written, unwritten and yet to be written Fae legends
and lore of galore.
The 'uncontested flumes' for sweet angelic essence.
The 'teachers' of wing resonance, music and harmonics of flight.
The 'doctors' and 'unwavering caretakers' of Unicorn medicine.
The 'den mothers' of triumphant mischief.
The rightful 'architects' of winged light sacred geometry.
The 'creative dancers' of ionized spark lights.
You are healing, beautified luminosity; the authentic fireworks of nature;
and the ascended breath of flight, and flight of breath.
You are the sacred, unbroken marriage of magic and mysticism.
With kindness and gratitude, we ask for your dancing light guidance to
restore and replenish the sacred hues of love, inspiration, passion,
playfulness and kindness."
Amor Vincit Omnia – Love Conquers All

Kind Karma Quote #112

Planet Kind Karma® Initiative
Crystals

"Crystals are magic, soothing LIGHT elixirs for our emotions, nervous system, physical body and energy body. They are alchemical tools gifted to us by Mother Earth and the Higher Power."

Kind Karma Quote #113

Kind Karma® Community Rocks!
(Awakening & Healing the Collective
Community Consciousness)

Using Crystals for Kindness
*"When used properly, crystals embolden us to rise to
our highest potential and vibration, while anchoring
us with the root energies of Mother Earth."*

Kind Karma Quote #114

Kind Karma® Community Rocks! (Awakening & Healing the Collective Community Consciousness)

"When you learn the 'Crystal Source Code' – the language of the crystals – you can communicate with the living essence that dwells inside each crystal."

Kind Karma Quote #115

Kind Karma® Kids R Key Initiative

(Empowering our youth for a positive, high vibration future)
"Children are our sustained breath, and future heart-light of compassion, peace and kindness."

Kind Karma Quote #116

Awaken with Meditation

*"Every mindful breath we take reshapes and enhances the inner
landscape of our body."*

Kind Karma Quote #117

Awaken with Meditation

"Meditation is not zeroing out, it's zeroing in."

Kind Karma Quote #118

Awaken with Meditation

"Meditation is the art of letting go, not the art of holding on."

Kind Karma Quote #119

Awaken with Meditation

"Awaken with Meditation is a journey of a lifetime, and each inner journey begins with the first mindful breath."

Kind Karma Quote #120

Awaken with Meditation

"Mantra – sound vibrations, helps with achieving mind over matter, while delineating a path to self-discovery, and self-concept clarity."

Kind Karma Quote #121

Awaken with Meditation

"It's helpful to view each meditation session as an inner peace destination, and not as a difficult perfection practice."

Kind Karma Quote #122

Awaken with Meditation

"When you meditate,
softly close your eyes.
Tune inward.
Feel the inner calm, the silence.
Allow your heart to open,
and breathe into its infinite spaciousness.
Search the stillness inside you.
Bathe in your awakened compassion.
Inspire love.
Radiate kindness.
And, succumb to the warmth of self-love,
and the jubilance of God."

Kind Karma Quote #123

Awaken with Meditation

"Stillness is the death of restlessness. It transforms an uncomfortable body and an unsettled mind into ashes that can be easily scattered along the vast sea of tranquility."

Kind Karma Quote #124

Awaken with Meditation

"There's nothing to do or fix in meditation, there's only let it be and let it go."

Kind Karma Quote #125

Awaken with Meditation

"There is no failure in meditation, unless you are too attached to the outcome or the experiences that sometimes arise from it."

Kind Karma Quote #126

Awaken with Meditation

"We practice meditation until it no longer becomes a 'practice'. At that point, there is no more 'try'. There is no more, 'I have to do it'. Or, 'I have to fit it in'. Through the commitment of a steady practice, it becomes a seamless fabric texture of... 'just is'; not who we aren't or weren't. It becomes unrecognizable or inextinguishable because it becomes 'who we are'. Accordingly, it becomes the lengthiness of our breath, and the scope resonance of our beingness. We no longer have to get there or anywhere, for that matter, because we have already arrived."

Kind Karma Quote #127

Awaken with Meditation

"Simultaneously, as we cultivate and expand the positive qualities in our life, we should also take time out to sit with this newly found stillness and silence. When we practice both of these aspects – action and stillness, we are always reminding ourselves they are inseparable. Like two wings of a bird, both are needed to launch a successful, sustainable flight."

Kind Karma Quote #128

Awaken with Meditation

"When settling in your meditation posture, let your body reflect the state of mind you are attempting to achieve."

Kind Karma Quote #129

Awaken with Meditation

Humpty Dumpty Had No ZEN - "Mythos of H.D."
Humpty Dumpty sat on a wall,
{"not realizing He wore a fleeting shawl"}
Humpty Dumpty had a great fall;
{"because He seemingly thought He had it all"}
All the king's horses and all the king's men
{"the past the future now can only be truly then"}
Couldn't put Humpty together again.
{"with a futile effort because Humpty Dumpty
had no Zen"}

Kind Karma Quote #130

Kind Karma® Yoga

"Kind Karma® Yoga is about how far we can stretch our heart; not how far we can bend over to touch our toes."

Kind Karma Quote #131

Kind Karma® Yoga

"The beauty of Kind Karma® Yoga is that its openness comes from the heart; therefore, it's for everyone – no one is excluded."

Kind Karma Quote #132

Kind Karma® Yoga

"Did you know KINDNESS is great at YOGA and extremely flexible? It can stretch as far as your HEART can go."

Kind Karma Quote #133

Kind Karma® Yoga

"During yoga practice, our breathing lends itself to give our body its shape and support. When our body shape changes, the yoga pose becomes inherently different. When the yoga pose feels different, then an unexpected, unfiltered, authentic experience arises."

Kind Karma Quote #134

Kind Karma® Yin Yoga

"Kind Karma® Yin Yoga is a floor-based practice of meditation and mindfulness that provides the opportunity to 'shape' you into what you want to become. It allows you to become the best version of yourself, by offering you the opportunity to make a conscious decision to let go of what no longer serves you."

Kind Karma Quote #135

Awaken Qigong

"Awaken Qigong is a natural way to achieve vibrant health by awakening our self-healing ability and nourishing our body, mind and spirit. Its core tenet is self-love, reminding us that we are the very best doctors of our own soul care."

Kind Karma Quote #136

Awaken Qigong

"A calm mind paired with a relaxed body increases energy (chi) circulation and opens energy pathways (meridians). This harmony can be achieved by allowing the natural flow of our breath to awaken the forgotten parts of our energy body."

Kind Karma Quote #137

Awaken Qigong

"Visualization and imagination are potent techniques to awaken the mind-body-energy connection."

Kind Karma Quote #138

Awaken Qigong

"I am Chi. Chi is Me."

Kind Karma Quote #139

Kind Karma® Reiki

"The expression of Reiki is found not so much in the energy itself, but the 'human' action of love, kindness, compassion, and empathy that fuels the Reiki energy."

Kind Karma Quote #140

Kind Karma® Reiki

"Sending distant Reiki is possible because love, compassion and empathy are not confined, and can transcend time, space, distance and dimension."

Kind Karma Quote #141

5th Dimension

"Proclaim and engage your Soul Essence by embodying love, compassion, kindness, and humility. The lightwork can only begin if you are becoming."

Kind Karma Quote #142

Kind Karma Worldwide™

"My favorite 'kind' of karma is Kind Karma®!"

About the Author

Dean Telano, Ph.D., E-RYT 500, RCYT, RPYT, KKRGM-24 is the Founder of Kind Karma Worldwide™ & Kind Karma® Yoga. He is also the creator of Awaken Qigong & Awaken with Meditation.

Dean Telano is a former adjunct professor, author, exercise physiologist, meditation coach, and Gong Master. His MS degree in Exercise Physiology paved the path of extensive involvement in the health & fitness fields, nutrition, yoga, meditation, sound healing, and energy work for 40 years. Dean is a co-owner of a Yoga & Holistic Center where he contributes his wealth of knowledge by teaching and leading courses, events, and classes that emphasize wellness as a holistic integration of the physical, mental, and spiritual well-being. As well, he travels to give lectures, workshops, and events to support his humanitarian nonprofit organization, Kind Karma Worldwide™'s mission to raise the consciousness of humanity and increase the world's vibration.

Dean has been a Registered Yoga Teacher with Yoga Alliance since 2001. His yoga training and study includes Kind Karma® Yoga, Rahini Yoga®, Hatha, Kundalini, Vinyasa, Power, Raja, Kundalini Maha, Tibetan, Naam, Yin, MEM Gong Yoga, Restorative and Therapeutic Yoga, and Children's Yoga. He offers trainings and certifications to the public in Yoga, Meditation, Gong & Sound, Awaken with Meditation, Awaken Qigong, Crystal Healing, various Reiki Healing Courses including Crystal Reiki and Animal & Pet Reiki.

To learn more about Dr. Dean Telano, visit his website: https://www.deantelano.com

Made in the USA
Middletown, DE
09 April 2022